Single Ladies: Why You're Still Single

By: Marita Kinney

Pure Thoughts Publishing, LLC

I0169195

Respective authors own all copyrights not held by the publisher.

The information herein is offered for informational purposes solely, and is universal as so. The presentation of the information is without contract or any type of guarantee assurance.

The trademarks that are used are without any consent, and the publication of the trademark is without permission or backing by the trademark owner. All trademarks and brands within this book are for clarifying purposes only and are the owned by the owners themselves, not affiliated with this document.

ISBN: 978-1-943409-05-1

Table of Contents

Intro

If you're reading this book right now, I would first like to thank you for exploring your current situation and having the courage to do some self- discovery. I'm pretty sure that you're sick and tired of being single by now and maybe, just maybe you will find some helpful information in this book. Well honey you're in luck. I'm confident that I can offer some great insight during this reading experience. Some of the things mentioned in this book will make you feel uncomfortable, however the topics are all written out of love. Now, I understand that you probably wouldn't buy a book like this, or it may be a little embarrassing. Let's forget all of that. As you read this book just look at it like this, we're just two friends talking and drinking coffee discussing our love lives. Yep! There's nothing greater than to love and to be loved. Everyone wants to experience true love at least once in a lifetime. The key to finding that love is within you, I'm just that friend in your life that helps you to see things from a different perspective.

Allow me to offer some of my background with you. I can relate to you and your singleness to a certain degree. However I didn't stay single very long. Now before you go and request a refund for purchasing this book, ask yourself this question, "Do you want to learn from another single woman or a married woman?" I hope you decided to learn from someone married. It's important to learn from those individual who have already obtained the goal that you're trying to reach. That goes for anything in life. I have had different levels of being single. I'll explain later on in this book. The techniques I'm going to share with you can be applied to almost anyone in any situation. I'm referring to the single mothers, divorced, widowed, independent, and vulnerable woman. At some point in my life I was all of these types of a woman, literally. Although my situations were not ideal, nor desired by men, I still was able to get married and have a healthy relationship. I'm going to share with you the good, bad, ugly, and the mistakes that I've made. To be honest, you probably have more of an advantage than I had. I'll show you how to use your current season of singleness to your advantage. Let's dive right in.

Whatever you do, don't lose hope. The change starts within you. There is no need to feel helpless, your blessing may be on the other side of you. Feel free to use the table of contents and skip to the sections that interest you the most. Enjoy!!!
Disclaimer: This book is not written for those women who want a boyfriend. If you want a boyfriend and nothing more, please understand that you're still a single woman with a boyfriend. Let me help you out. When you file your taxes with the IRS and you file *single*, boyfriend or not, you're still single. If you're not married you're single. This book is designed for those individuals you truly no longer want to be single and desire to one day be a wife. Because I'm a woman, I write from a female's point of view. Also because I'm a Christian I write from a Bible perspective. Either way I believe that you'll get something from this book that will assist you on your journey to obtaining true love. Enjoy!

Chapter 1: What do you really want?

This is a common single issue. There of hundreds of thousands of women who cannot determine what they truly want out of life. I'm referring to those indecisive women. Women who are so unsure of themselves that men cannot read them. What signals are you giving off? Do you really want to be married or do you enjoy being single? As women we have gotten it all wrong. No one told us the truth about being a wife or becoming one. Most of us were always taught to look for what a man can do for us. When in reality the strongest marriages are servers of love and each other, displaying a, "What can I do for you mentality." Is that what you want? Can you handle putting your own selfish desires aside to please and serve someone else?

Knowing what you want is important. However understanding what you want is a vital missing piece that few woman get without guidance. I cannot tell you how many woman thought that they wanted to be married, and are now secretly miserable and resenting their life. The problem is that they never truly understood marriage, therefore wanted something without fully understanding its purpose. Anything that is misused will cause frustration. Let's first understand how marriage is supposed to be used and what purpose it serves.

As a Christian we are taught that Adam existed before Eve. If you're not a Christian, don't worry. You'll simply learn how we as Christians believe and it will be pretty cool. I have learned about other beliefs although I don't practice their faith. I just love to be educated. Ok, moving on! Back to Adam. Anyway, he was in charge on naming all of the animals and of course realized that the animals had a mate. He began to yearn for a significate other too.

Genesis 2:18
The LORD God said, "It is not good for the man to be alone. I will make a helper suitable for him."

So again I ask, "Do you know what you want?" Do you want to be his helper that is suitable for *him*? That means that you have to be what *he* is looking for. Every man may not need the same thing in a woman. Not all men have the same needs. So you cannot be every man's desire. Although you may be God's gift to a man…but not all men. So if you're walking around thinking that you're God's gift to men, you're thinking will defiantly keep you single.

You Cannot Be God's Gift to Men

Instead of focusing on all men, turn your attention to you. Develop your skills and abilities so that when the time comes for you to cross paths with" your Adam" he'll be able to recognize you. If you're imitating anyone instead of being yourself, you run the risk of deceiving a companion who may later resent you. What do you want? Do you want to be yourself or fool someone into loving a fraudulent version of you? Deciding what you really want is the key. Do you want to be a helpmate or are you selfishly looking for someone to meet all of your needs. Of course we all want our own needs met. But when it's done selfishly, you're no longer considering your significate other's needs, you just want what you want at the expense of disregarding everyone else. If this is describing you, you may want to reconsider if you really want to be married. When you chose to enter into a relationship, you're simply willing to give of yourself completely. The same is true for that man.

Not focusing on what you can get from that person. Instead you should be asking, "What can I give, what do I have to offer?" Can you handle being selfless? The great thing about being selfless is that, the more you give the more you receive. When you commit to loving and serving, that same love, honor, and serving will be returned back to you. You have to teach others how to treat you. If you want to be loved unconditionally, you have to learn how to love others unconditionally. Is that what you want?

Is Marriage What You Really Want?

Do you really want to spend the rest of your life with someone, or are you just in love with the idea of getting married?

It may seem like a harsh question, but it's something worth asking yourself. If you're suddenly feeling unsure, read on. This book may help you find the answer to that question. What follows are steps that won't just help you get an awesome man to marry you. It will also take you on a journey to discover who you really are, what you really want, and what to do while waiting for Mr. Right.

Chapter 2: Marriage Mindset

Obtain a marriage mindset

If you want to buy a car or the latest gadget, you're bound to do an extensive amount of research to get the best possible product and deal out there. If you're willing to put in that much effort because you'll be spending a lot of money buying something, it makes perfect sense to put in even more effort to look into what marriage really is. After all, you'll be spending a lot of money on it too, plus you're going to commit your life to it.

Before you go on this quest to prepare yourself to be with Mr. Right, you have to know what you're getting into.

What does it mean to be married? What work goes into "for better or worse, for richer or poorer, in sickness and in health, 'til death do us part."?

Are you in it for keeps, or are you holding on to those divorce and annulment cards *just in case*?

Yes, marriage is supposed to be something romantic – something sweet, magical and special. Those are definitely a few of the many wonderful qualities of marriage. However, it is also a lot of hard work. It may take a lot of time to prepare for a wedding, but it should ideally take longer to prepare for marriage. Most women spend their time planning a wedding before they even get a proposal, forget that…..before they even get a man. While deep down inside you may not be Mrs. Right for your imagery Mr. Right. Are you complete and ready to merge your life with that man of your dreams? Besides, the last thing you need is for Mr. Right to be attached to you and all of your incompleteness demanding that he make you happy. Let's be honest, that's a lot of responsibility to bestow on a person. That would mean that you're giving someone control over your life to make you happy or unhappy. Marriage takes a lot of work and most of the work is for you to do. You're responsible for *you*. At the end of the day you must consider who you are and what you have to bring to the table. So let's dive into some deep marriage mindset stuff.

Here are a few practical things you can to do obtain a marriage mindset:

- Talk to your married friends and ask them about the work that goes into a marriage. This my dear will go beyond the wedding day, trust me.
- Read books on marriage, as well as those that discuss the differences of men and women.
- Read blogs and articles online about the challenges of marriage.
- Become what you desire to be. If you want to be married you should let your life reflect that transition. Wives are wives before they get married. Practice a daily routine that mirrors the wife that you hope to be.

After doing these, you'll learn that most of the time, it isn't a walk in the park. You might learn about really challenging stuff. Learning isn't meant to discourage you. It's supposed to prepare, challenge, and excite you for what's to come.

When you get to know the stories of real-life married couples, you'll see how beautiful marriage is. It is amazing to find out how each person has grown through both good and tough times. Do not ponder on advice from you *single friends*. Sorry, but they're single. I challenge you to find a mentor. Look to someone who is married and who you can trust to help groom you. Single women think differently than married women. It's true and you have to learn how to consider someone other than yourself to succeed in getting married.

Chapter 3: To Be Married, Why?

Decide why you want to get married

Now that you've discovered and learned what really goes into marriage, have you decided if you still want to say "I do" to someone someday? If the answer to that question is yes, the next question is "why do you want to get married?"

If you rely on fantasies (especially in terms of what marriage is), there'd be a big chance you'll end up pulling out your divorce card really fast. However, if you know the reason why you want to get married, there's a bigger chance you'll keep the commitment you make on your wedding day.

Write down all the reasons why you want to be married. Some ladies journal about this and it's a good idea. Marriage is an act of serving. Are you considering what you can do and offer a husband? Or are you focused on what he can potentially do and provide for you? Back to the marriage mindset, you must be willing to focus on what you're willing to do and give your future husband. I true marriage is about giving, it's the most selfless act that can dedicate to doing. It's a commitment to serving and loving someone even when you don't want to. You must be committed to the hard times and fighting through the toughest days. Can you do that? Can you love someone even when you feel like they don't deserve it anymore? Ask yourself these types of questions and make your list based on the reality of marriage and not its fantasy.

Chapter 4: Be Ms. Right

When we were kids, we often fantasized about our prince charming. We want nothing but the best. Well, who wouldn't? However, are YOU already the absolute Ms. Right for your Mr. Right? Allow me to answer that question for you. Probably not! In today's world we as women can get so distracted with our day-to-life. We all want the perfect man and yet we're nowhere near to being perfect. It's not fair to want someone with qualities that you have yet to possess for yourself. It's crazy to want a man who drives a nice car and your car stays in the shop and barely runs. You want to man with good credit, but bill collectors are calling your phone day and night. Why would a man with good credit want an irresponsible wife who cannot pay bills on time? Exactly, he wouldn't. You must become who you desire to have. Once you start to become Mrs. Right, the right man will admire the likeness and will automatically have something in common with you. If you enjoy working out, chances are that you'll have a physically fit man interested in you. However, you can't get upset if sloppy men are approaching you, what does that say about you?

Singleness does NOT EQUAL Loneliness.
Men are looking for Mrs. Right, just like you're hoping that Mr. Right will find you. A lot of women make the mistake of being TOO OVERLY OCCUPIED. Yep! It's true. You can be your own worst enemy and a distraction for men. We as women have no idea what we have become in the eyes of men. Men want us to be available. What's stopping you from being available and approachable? Is it your phone? Your daily drama? Or is it your friends or work? If you're overly preoccupied men will not approach you. Are you causing yourself to remain single?

Mrs. Right will know how to balance her life and leave room for the man of her dreams. Sometimes woman are guilty of staying busy to prevent themselves from becoming lonely. It sounds good, but if that describes you….I have one question, "Are you still single?" I'm not trying to be harsh. I'm just being honest. Woman who are too busy, also appear to be too busy for a love life in the eyes of men. Do you have time to be courted? Do you have time to be a wife and possibly a mother? Use your time wisely. Remember that you don't have to take up every second of the day trying to stay busy. It's important to know how to be *with yourself* and not *by yourself*.

Mrs. Right will be confident. Most men don't really care how you look. I can't believe I just said that. Well it's true whenever your confident being in your own skin. Men are attracted to confidence more than image. There's nothing worse than being a beautiful woman who lacks self-confidence. Have you ever seen ugly women that are also married? My point exactly. Inner beauty is so much prevalent than outer beauty. Who you are at the core is what will make you desirable to men. Don't compare yourself to other women. Embrace who you are and what you have to offer.

Get yourself together.

Chapter 5: Get to know yourself all over again

Experiences change us. This is true, especially if you've been in several relationships or if you have been traveling a lot. Get to know yourself the same way you would get to know a guy.

What are your interests? What kind of movies do you like? What kind of books do you read? What kind of music do you enjoy? What's your dream holiday? What is your dream job? Where do you want to be five or ten years from now? What are your fears, and would you like to overcome those fears? If you know who you are, you'll know what you want. There's nothing worse than to meet a guy and you're completely lost. You have to know who you are. It's crucial. No man wants to be with a woman who is in la la land. If you're lost spiritually, emotionally, and mentally, you are literally not Mrs. Right, you are actually a bad situation gone wrong. I'm not trying to be blunt but the only man that you're going to get in that state of mind is a LOST MAN.

We all have goals in life and sometimes, we put ourselves last on our list of priorities. How can you do anything effectively when the person that you're neglecting is *you*? Investing in your personal growth, strengthening your weaknesses, and becoming a better person overall should be your number one priority. This will result in extraordinary results in your life. In order to become the very best *you* that you can possibly be, you need to first look at your weaknesses. Evaluate your life and determine what areas need improvement. Although this can be a difficult process, be honest with yourself and know your starting point in order to see how much work you need to do to get to where you desire be.

Bridging the gap of where you are and where you would like to be can sometimes be overwhelming and even disappointing. However, I encourage you not to worry about how long it will take you to arrive to that desired position in life. I challenge you to enjoy your journey. When you look back and see how far you've come, I guarantee that you'll feel such an accomplishment within yourself. This will also become the motivation to keep moving you forward.

Chapter 6: First Impression

As most of you all know, first impressions are essential when getting someone's attention or their perception being formed about you. One of the biggest mistakes I see every day is women trying too hard to get attention. Dressing provocatively is not the attention you want to get. Keep your boobs put away, your butt covered, and your thighs hidden away. If you have a nice shape it will be obvious no matter what. You want to get a commitment that hopefully leads to marriage not a booty call or friends with benefits relationship. Real men want a woman that knows how to wear her hats appropriately. There is a time and place for everything. The secret is to attract men who are looking for wives. You have to be a wife before you get married. Of course not to him, but I'm referring to the demeanor you have from afar. Are you representing someone that a man would be proud to take home to meet his mother?

KICA- Keep it Classy Always. Dress like you're taken. It will be intriguing when they find out that you're single yet carry yourself with such poise. Demand respect from men by how well you treat yourself. When you honor yourself and your body from the way you dress, you send off a signal that you're worth being taken seriously. This is all from your first impression. It's hard to change someone's perspective of you after a first impression had been established.

Some woman work really hard to impress men by trying to look sexy, not realizing that they look desperate instead of looking desirable for companionship. Please don't make this mistake. You cannot buy sexy. Being sexy is a state of being. It's not found in your clothes, hair, lashes, or stilettos. Sexiness is found in your walk, your body language, your confidence, and smile. A true woman will get the attention of a man because he will notice her value and what she can add to his life. Men want to be inspired by their woman in some way, shape, or form. As a helpmate, you have to be identified as their support or other half to assist him in reaching his greatest potential. Remember, different men may need different things from a wife. I heard a saying that was so interesting to me, "Women are the choosers and men are the deciders." If you think about it you'll realize that it's certainly true. Men decide to marry the woman, and the woman chooses to date the man she's most interested in. That's just something to ponder on.

Anyway, back to being sexy. Men want a challenge because a challenge is sexy. Discovering who a woman is at her core and having to work for it is ideal for a man finding a wife. If you're a woman that a man doesn't have to work hard for anything with you, chances are that he may not take you serious enough to marry and will overlook your value. You have to leave some mystery to you to keep his attention. I'm married and I'm still revealing things that my husband appreciates about me. We are continuously learning each other, now that's sexy.

How many times have you heard the statement, "Dress for success?" Well it's the same principle for attracting your mate. Dress in a manner that will show him your intentions without having to say a word. What does your appearance say about you?

You desire to be a wife
You desire to have beautiful children
You're bitter
You want every man to look at your physical attributes
You're tired and could less about life
You don't have time for a man

You're all about pleasing yourself
You don't care about your appearance anymore

Don't get me wrong you should care about your appearance at all times. You never know who or when you could run into someone. However make sure that you're dressed appropriately for wherever you're going. Please, please, comb your hair, smell good, get dress for the day, put on your make-up if you choose, and most importantly put on a smile. Present yourself pleasant and approachable at all times. It's not attractive for you to wear a frown as if you're on your menstrual every day of the week. Mean looking woman send off the impression that she's scorn, hates life, bitter, and would make a man's life hell. Practice smiling every day, you'll feel better throughout the day too. Also, look up some images online to give you an idea of what looks inspire you. Last and not least, look up at pictures of yourself and determine what you like and what you may want to change.

Chapter 7: Forgive and Move Forward

     If you've ever had your heart broken you may be suffering from PTSD (Post Traumatic Stress Syndrome Disorder). This doesn't just occur in military members, but can occur in anyone who has suffered from serve emotional trauma. Believe it or not, you can wear this hurt all over you for years. Getting over a past relationship is critical. Have you ever been in a fight? Well I have and oh my goodness the adrenaline is none like no other. Once your adrenaline kicks in you cannot feel anything. You instantly shift into survivor mode. This is true for other tragic events that occur in our lives. You go into survivor mode, simply trying to make it through another day. During a fight adrenaline gives you everything you need to fight and to defend yourself. After the fight ends and things settle down, you suddenly begin to notice the bruises and scars. In fact, you don't know how badly you're hurt until the fight well over and done. Guess what? Relationships have the same tendency to have that same effect on us. Sometimes you cannot recognize how hurt you are until someone other than yourself points it out. If you enter into another relationship too soon, the person who points it out may be the man who realizes that you're too broken to be with. Hurt people hurt other people. Chances are if you're hurt from a past relationship you could end up being the woman who sub cautiously hurts others. You become a red flag woman. When men notice how hurt you are, they may see a red flag to leave your crazy self alone. Please don't be offended, I'm telling you this out of love.

     If you feel that you have been severely hurt from past relationships I suggest that you begin to talk about it. There are counselors, church leaders, and life coaches that are trained to help you overcome past hurts and embrace a brighter future. It will take a lot of courage on your end, but the happiness of your life may be counting on this change from you. As a board certified life coach, you can contact me at www.MaritaKinney.com or another qualified professional. Either way, I encourage you to give yourself permission to heal from that hurt and encounter the life you truly deserve.

Forgiving yourself and others is the first step in order to move forward in your life. You have to decide to step into another dimension of your life. Each time you dwell on your hurtful past you give "the past" permission to become part of your present moment. Your brain and emotions will react as if it's happening all over again. All the feelings associated with that painful moment all come running back into your day. Be determined to declare that your past is your past and will no longer dictate how you will feel today. Take the authority over your past. Choose to forgive even if you don't feel like it. If you're waiting until you feel like it, you'll be waiting a lifetime. Forgive now and your feelings will soon follow your decision.

Chapter 8: Improve Yourself

Think of the areas you need to improve on as a person Now that you know your good qualities and interests, it's time to dig a little deeper. What are the qualities you want to improve on? Do you have any issues that would affect your future relationship? Do you have any unresolved concerns with those around you? Are you carrying a heavy heart because of something? Has anyone described you in a negative way, and do you think there is any truth to what was said?

A lot of ladies in relationships are often heard complaining about the negative qualities of their boyfriends (or husbands). Unfortunately, most of those ladies fail to see their own flaws and mistakes. It will be better to enter a relationship once you've ended your internal struggles.

Of course, the goal is not to be perfect, but at least you're doing something to be a better person slowly (but surely). Don't expect your knight in shining armor to save you from whatever issues you have. If he finds out that you're willing to acknowledge your issues and do something about them, he'll definitely love you more as he realizes how brave you are.

It's amazing how small steps don't feel like you're making much progress at all. The small steps, over time, will become one huge step in which we might not have been able to take otherwise. Don't look at the big picture as an obstacle. Sometimes, looking at the big picture can be intimidating; therefore, we procrastinate to make the changes necessary in order to better ourselves. Stop looking at the big picture, especially if you're easily intimidated by hard work and effort. Perseverance is the key to making the change that you want to see in your life.

You must be determined to become a better person and commit to doing whatever it takes to make that thought a reality. You can keep the big picture in mind, but don't focus on it. Focus on the small steps that are necessary for you to complete your goal. As a life coach, there are various areas in your life that are supposed to make you feel complete. Whenever someone is lacking in an area of fulfillment, they seem to shortchange the quality of life that they could possibly live. The areas in life that make people complete are the following:

Career
Significant other
Family
Friends
Physical health and well-being
Emotional health and well-being
Physical environment
Finances
Spirituality/religion
Education/personal growth
Fun and leisure
Lifestyle
Balance in life

On a scale of 1 to 10, in the areas above, indicate where you are in each level of satisfaction. Choose the lowest level of satisfaction and write down the things that you don't like about it. Then, write down what you would like to change about that particular area of life. Becoming the very best *you* that you can possibly be is highly encouraged. Prioritize the lowest number that you rated yourself and focus on improving that area. You may also want to focus on the things that you need to do in order to turn that lowest number into a satisfactory 10.

I encourage you to do a self-evaluation. In every area mentioned in this article, honestly rate yourself to see what areas could use improvement. It's never too late to become the very best person that you can be. Once you improve the unsatisfactory ratings in your life, you'll begin to notice yourself transforming within. Sometimes, we can lack the motivation that's necessary for us to change. If that is the case for you, just remember what kind of life you'll have if you *never* make the change. If you're not okay with the result, dedicate your time to investing in yourself.

Love your imperfections

Learning to love you means loving the things about yourself that you consider to be a flaw and cannot change. You may be struggling with negative history from past relationships, your family background, or even becoming a single parent. But it's these things that make you who you are. Once you're able to embrace your negative views of yourself or circumstances, you can begin to love all the things that have occurred in your life. Once you do this, others will learn to love you—including your imperfections—as well.

Chapter 9 List it

Make a list and check it more than twice
The more you know yourself, the more you'll know what kind of guy you'd want to partner up with and marry. List down all the qualities you want in a husband. Be as specific as you can get. I remember doing this and my list was very long. What? I felt as though I had a lot to offer and I wanted someone who could bring the same to the table.

Remember, you have to make sure that the list is a reflection of you are. Think of the kind of person who'll complement you perfectly. Try not to focus too much on what you want in a guy. Instead, think hard abut the kind of person you would work best with as a team.

Think of everyday life. Think of activities you'd want to do with your husband. Think of the adventures you'd want to share with him. One of the greatest things about marriage is having someone to share experiences with, so imagine all the fun you'd have with your husband.

If you like going to concerts, it would be great to have someone who enjoys going to such events too (or at least someone who's excited to give it a shot). If you like to cook, it would be great to have someone who has an adventurous palate. If fitness is important to you, it would be better to have a partner who sees its importance too.

That list could go on and on, but always try to ask yourself why you wrote down each quality. Is it a negotiable quality, or is it totally non-negotiable (like having the same beliefs or faith)?

Remember, it isn't all about one's romantic qualities. A husband and wife must function as a team. So, you're looking for a team mate, someone you can conquer the world with.

Chapter 10: Be Flexible

Keep that list safe, but don't obsess about it!

Don't get caught up in "the list." Don't go carrying it around ticking item after item as soon as you meet someone new. Since you've already set your standards in your head and you more or less know what kind of person you'd want to invest your time in, you can relax and say no to all the "wrong" guys.

The list you just made isn't the final say on what guy you're going to let into your life. Look at it as a guide. Those are standards you feel you deserve. Don't treat it as an absolute checklist. Keep an open mind, but don't make compromises when it comes to your self-worth.

If you're seeing one red flag after another and you can't seem to say no to this new guy, go ahead and think about everything you've learned in this journey so far. Go back to the qualities of the partner you'd want to spend the rest of your life with, and recall why you thought of those qualities in the first place. Afterwards, ask yourself if you want to give all those up just because this new guy seems fun and interesting, aside from making you feel warm and fuzzy every now and then.

Chapter 11: Don't go searching for him

He'll find you. He's supposed to!

Proverbs 18:22
Whoever gets a wife gets a good thing, and has the approval of the Lord.

By this stage, you know who you are, and you've been working on your issues. You love and respect yourself more than ever. You also know the type of guy you're willing to invest your precious time in. Looks like you're in a pretty good place. Now all you have to do is wait for him while you're having the time of your life. Enjoy the freedom that you have because the moment he finds you, it'll be a totally different "season" altogether.

Go out with your girlfriends. Do the things that drive your passion. If you love what you do, you'd definitely look happier and lovelier. If you love dogs and would want to be with someone who loves dogs just as much as you do, hang out at the dog park. That way, you'll have greater chances of attracting someone likeminded.

Remember though, you're doing all this for you, and not because you're looking for Mr. Right. You'll be fooling no one, but yourself, if you're doing one activity after another just to try to attract men. When you're living your life to the fullest while waiting, there'll be no regrets in the end. Whatever you're doing now won't seem useless.

It's easy for someone to love you, when you first love yourself. This sounds easy, but believe me, learning to love yourself can be very difficult. We all want someone to love, but oftentimes we don't extend love to ourselves. Many people end up in dead end relationships due to low standards stemming from low self-esteem. However, when you choose to love yourself, those standards naturally become higher because you see yourself worthy of the love of someone special.

Let love look for you

Many unhealthy relationships develop because the woman was looking for love instead of allowing it to find her. Instead of looking for love, spend more time preparing yourself for that special someone. Once you love yourself and are at peace with who you are, love will find you.

Here are some simple steps that will help you learn to love "YOU":

• Accept what you cannot change.
• Forgive your past mistakes.
• Realize that there is only one you and you are unique; do not compare yourself to anyone else.
• Embrace your past as a learning experience, not as a failure.
• Fall in love with your scars, internally and externally. Your scars make you who you are today. They hold a story and once you're comfortable revealing them, you'll realize their strength.
• If you have children, love the accomplishment of becoming a parent. Your children are your legacy. If someone really loves you, they will also love your children, not just tolerate them.
• Treat yourself well. Take pride in who you are and where you have come from.
• Respect yourself and others will do the same.

The good news is loving yourself is the key to attracting a good man. Some of you may think that this is old-fashioned. However, if you're honest with yourself for a moment you will see that it all starts with you. When you invest time and energy into yourself, there is a certain level of self-esteem that forms. The confidence that you send off is noticeable to everyone around you.

Chapter 12: Now What?

If you think you've met the one, don't go after him

So, it seems Mr. Right has finally found you. Sparks are flying everywhere. You may be all giddy and excited, but don't throw everything you've worked for out the window. Stay calm, your self-respect will keep him interested.

Try your best not to say "yes" to an offer to go out on the same day he invites you. Eventually, there'll be a time for spontaneous dates. Now is not the time. During your first few dates, send the message that he has to respect your time too. Don't be scared to lose him. If a man is really interested in you, he'll be willing to wait. If he doesn't, then it's clearly his loss – not yours. Besides, the last thing you'd want is to be with someone who isn't patient and doesn't respect your time.

Don't plan your dates. Let him lead. If he asks what you feel like doing, you can either answer with "surprise me" or give a few general suggestions. Let him do most, if not all, of the planning. You're showing him a lot of respect by doing so. Simply put, remember to choose a man you can trust and respect.
You're setting the tone for your marriage the moment you meet and start going out. Allow your man to do the hard work. Men were wired to be hunters, so let him hunt for you. Men love to be challenged. You'll be doing him a huge favor if you let him wear the pants in the relationship.

If you'd do everything for him, making sure that he doesn't face any kind of difficulty when you're still dating, imagine what your life will be like when you're married. He'll have far more responsibilities when he becomes your husband and, eventually, the father to your child.

So many women complain about one thing – their husbands aren't acting like men. It is best, however, to examine what tone the woman has set at the start of the relationship. Has she taken the lead in everything? When a man doesn't seem to have a voice in the relationship, you have to find out who switched off his "microphone".

Women are so used to taking charge of every situation they're in. They have the tendency to have such a tight grip on life's steering wheel. If you were the man in that relationship, why would you bother to take the lead?

There's nothing wrong with having a guy do what he's supposed to do. When you aren't together, be the independent woman that you are. When you're together, it's time to rest, relax, and let him pursue you. This doesn't give you the right to boss him around though. Always keep in mind that the both of you are a team. You've got your role, and he has his. Practice working as a team from day one.

Chapter 13: Time

Enjoy the time you spend together, but don't make him your world

You had a life before you started dating. You're not about to drop all of that, right? Do the things you both enjoy. Try new activities together. Enjoy getting to know each other while having the time of your lives.

It may seem like you're inseparable, but don't forget to give him some space. You can't be in his face all the time. Men need to go back into their caves every so often. Your man needs to recharge and do his own thing too. Giving him the freedom to do so will show how much you trust and respect him. When he's back in his cave, keep yourself busy. Don't call or text him every ten minutes to ask him what he's doing.

Do you remember all the things that used to take up your time before you met him? Keep at least a few of those activities in your schedule. The space is healthy for both of you.

Dating someone doesn't mean you have to stop learning new skills or taking up classes. You're on a continuous journey to be the best you. Your desire to grow as a person will make him respect you even more. Besides, the breathing space you'd give him will make him yearn for you even more.

This time is extremely important in a relationship. By this time you should be able to talk about hot topics. Hot topics are conversations that give you some insight to the relationships future. This is where most women go wrong. The best advice I can give you, is it listen carefully. If a man tells you that he isn't ready for anything serious, well listen to him. Believe what he is sharing with you and don't waste your time on someone who does not have marriage in mind. Respect the truth that is being told to you. Please don't try to convince a man to marry you. That's desperate and plain out sad. Have some dignity. A man should want to marry you but be bribed into it. Whenever you force marriage on a man who isn't ready for it, resentment builds and misery grows. The point is to make sure that the man you're seeing has a marriage mind set as well. I remember hearing someone say," Women are the choosers and men are they deciders." Actually that's true. Men decide if they want to marry or not. In fact that means that most men take marriage more serious than women. Yep, that's what I said. Most men would rather stay single than to settle being married to just any woman. Whereas some women are so desperate to get married, they'd marry anyone. That's sad, but true. Don't settle for anything less than love. Several men have told me that, a man knows within 6-12 months if the woman he's dating *is the one*. If he doesn't decide to marry her it's because he afraid that there is someone better. Often times because of that fear, men are afraid to commit and the relationship eventually goes sour. Of course that woman moves on with her broken heart and another man marries her. She then is referred to as "the one who got away." Either way, a man knows who he should have committed to. You cannot force his heart to love you.

If marriage is what you want and obviously it is because you're reading this book, don't waste your time on men who are afraid of a commitment. If he refers to you as his friend, don't make it more than it is. YOU'RE HIS FRIEND. So many women fall victim to overly analyzing a "friendship." Don't go over and beyond trying to change the dynamics of the friendship. Instead allow things to happen naturally. Leave some mystery about yourself. If you treat

every man you're interested in like "your king" what will you have
to offer "your husband?"

Chapter 14: Look Beyond Yourself

Be good to him and he'll want to take you home to mom

Before any woman came into the picture, your boyfriend's mom was there first. She took care of him the best possible way she could. One of her greatest fears is for her son to end up with someone who won't respect and support him. It's something she's done all her life, and she'd like to see someone continue doing exactly that to her son.

If you treat your man well with so much respect, he'll want his family to meet you. He'd be confident that you're going to treat them the same way. If you're a delight to be with and if you make each other happy, he'd want to make you meet his family and friends. For sure, he'd be proud to introduce this beautiful and interesting woman to the world.

Chapter 15: Believe in his dreams and potential

No man would want to spend the rest of his life with someone who looks down on him and his dreams. It's a good sign to be with a man who has dreams. Remember, you're a team and, most likely, you're going to be part of whatever dream he has. Your job as a couple is to support each other. You're supposed to be his number one fan and cheerleader. His plan may not always work out. However, since you've been there for him since day one, it'll encourage him to get back up and try even harder.

If your man is satisfied because he is able to go after his dreams and maximize his potentials, he'd be a happier boyfriend, husband, and father.

Let me tell you about the story of a woman who is successful in her career. She has always been on top of her game. She's with a guy who has a stable job. He's equally successful and is supportive of whatever she does. One day he told her that he wants to quit his job to pursue a dream he always had. He chose to be completely honest with her and told her that it is going to be a huge risk, but he knows that it's going to make him happy.

Now let me paint two possible reactions to this situation. One type of woman would totally support her man's plan. She acknowledges that it really is a huge risk – knowing her partner's potential though, she's willing to take that dive with him. She sees it as an adventure they can both take. He can finally work on pursuing his dream, while she cheers him on and assures him that she will be there for him – no matter what.

The other type of woman would be extremely hesitant about this move. She may even disagree with him and discourage him. She thinks the risk isn't worth it. She'll reason out that he has a stable job and he's successful at it – so, why change the status quo? She ends up absolutely refusing to consider whatever potential the plan has. She may even go through the list of his many flaws in her eyes, which she thinks would prove her point.

What would you do in this certain situation? Would you be the first type of woman or the second one? If you aren't too sure of your answer, let me paint a different picture for you.
If you had a dream you wanted to pursue and you told your boyfriend (or husband) about it, how would you want him to react? Wouldn't you want him to support your dreams as well? If he absolutely says "no" to what you want, you'd feel like he didn't trust you and your potential. The first person you expected to support you turned out to be the first person to put you down. Now if you'd feel that way, don't you think your man would feel the same way?
It won't be always easy, but believing in your partner's potential and supporting him will always produce better results – compared to if your default reaction is to doubt and discourage him. If you don't trust him and his capabilities, why are you with him in the first place?

I'm going to have two scenarios with you. Have you ever seen the movie Soul Food? If not, I encourage you to watch it for this purpose. In that movie it shows how a marriage can do destroyed because the wife failed to believe in her husband's dream career. At the end of the day a man wants to feel supported by his wife. If no one believes in him it should be her. He desires for her to encourage him even after he stops believing in himself. A man desires for his wife to see his potential, to see what he cannot see due to fear and insecurities. If a man does not feel support from his wife, he will grow to resent her. A woman like that is not being his helpmate and serves no purpose for him. Remember he needs you to be, what he needs you to be. God designed you to be his helpmate not his critic. What you're not willing to do for your husband another woman is praying for the opportunity.

The other scenario is from a joke I heard that was on point for the purpose of having a helpmate, a cheerleader, and a supporter. A district attorney and his wife were walking down the street arm in arm on a cold winter day. They noticed a homeless wrapped in an old raggedy blanket begging for food. As they slowly approached the man, the husband laughed as he realized it was his wife old high school sweetheart. Her eyes filled with tears out of pity and disgust from her husband's reaction and lack of compassion. The husband looked at her and said, "Aren't you glad that you married me instead of him?" she replied, "Had I married him, he would have been the district attorney and you would have been homeless."
What a statement to make, wow. Well sadly it's true in most cases. A woman is to help her mate reach his greatest potential. Of course she can have dreams too, but her primary responsibility is to her husband.

Chapter 16: Finances

This is the last chapter and may be the most common issue single women are suffering from. Have your finances been keeping you single? Do not under estimate the power of money. If you have a lot of debt or mismanage your money, this could be a deal breaker. Men do not want to marry your bad money issues. Get your finances is order. Believe it or not, your money and spending habits say a lot about you. When I was a widow with three small children I had this area of finances in my favor which I'm sure made my situation look more appealing. I had an 820 FICO credit score, owned a home, and had no debt. I was a college graduate with absolutely no student loans. Although I had a rough past, I had goals and my future looked bright. You have to have something to offer. No one wants to inherit your debt. Now it's not just debt, but it's you being a responsible adult. If you have debt, do me and you a favor and pay your bills on time. Men will judge you based on your credit and financial situation. Some things in life you may have absolutely no control over, but other things can be controlled with time. Whenever there is a lack in finances you could feel extremely hopeless, but you still have control. That's right. You may need to just change your perspective in order to change your situation. Money is never the problem. Instead it's a mindset problem. Why do you think some people win the lottery and end up broke a year later? Their mentality was not ready to handle a large sum of money. Start to train your mind right for an increase in finances. Give yourself a money make over. Take responsibility for the debt that you owe. You have to think about the services and products that your collectors provided and begin to be thankful for it. Being thankful is the key to getting out of financial trouble. Gratitude produces riches while complaining does the opposite, it produces poverty. If you have enjoyed the benefits of having cable, hot water, electricity, going to college, and a warm place to stay, you may want to think twice at that bill with gratitude and pay it with pride.

Often times we struggle with financial priorities not the lack of having money. So many people have borrowed money from others because they chose to mismanage their paychecks then want someone to bail them out. Ladies this is not a book that is going to go into details regarding your spending habits or financial challenges, but I am encouraging you to get every aspect of your life together so that you're not hindering your own blessing.

Chapter 17: Types of Men

The Alpha Male

      Alpha men are very strong dominating men. These powerful men of influence are successful at whatever they do. He's the man that most men aspire to be. They want to be adored and much respected. They need a woman to support them and to be their biggest fan. It takes an equally strong woman to be on the arm. Their ideal wife is strong yet soft and gentle. A woman who does not mind him having his spotlight. He will put a lot of demands on his wife, most of them will be unspoken but expected. Alpha men are extremely confident, and take pride in who they are and what they have to offer. They tend to be the type of man who take care of their wife….if he feels respected and loved by her. Most woman would find it hard to be with such a man, but the rewards of loving him conditionally is often envied by other women. An Alpha man knows what he wants. He's focused, ambitious, has purpose, and is a champion. He can and will defend his home and family. He is the most desired among the other type of men. However, it takes a special kind of woman to meet his needs. He needs her undivided attention at all times.

The Nice Guy

The Push Over, Steady Man, also known as the nice guy. These men are typically laid back and tend to be attracted to more dominating women. They avoid arguments and drama, by allowing their wife to get her way. They are natural peace makers, although they have a voice and an opinion. They try to find common ground in their relationship. However the woman they're with catch a hard time by others. Women married to this type of man can frowned upon as being ungrateful, mean, overbearing, and controlling. Nice guys are known to be pleasers, caring, faithful, and providing, and serving. If you are a little bit selfish, you will appear to be the worse companion EVER. The good thing about the Steady Man is that they are extremely faithful when they feel appreciated. If they're single it's because some stupid ungrateful woman has left him go. Because most of these men have long term relationships and are content.

The Dreamer/Visionary

These men are extremely creative. They either make a lot of money or are broke. They also have a new idea and will spend their last dollar on it. Women who are with this type of men need to be easy going, full of life, and ready for and adventure. Offering stability will not be these men strongest attribute. But they will offer you a long of fun and spontaneous living. The other types of men may appear to be boring and predictable. Stable yes! But may not be as fun and romantic. Creative men are often dreamers. They have great ideas but sometimes lack the discipline to commit to it. They start things but never finish because they got another great idea. They are not the best providers for their family, but are loyal to a woman who supports their dreams. Dreams can do things in life with the right woman by their side. Their wife must be patient, understanding, supportive, adventurous, and not be materialistic.

Chapter 18: My Experience with Love

When it comes to love and relationships, many of us have failed terribly. I admit I have learned some hard lessons and have bumped my head more than once, trying to figure out this thing we call love. One of the reasons we struggle with relationships is simply because there are issues that we often battled within ourselves. It's hard to love someone when you struggle with loving yourself.

Over the years I have met so many people that admit to their past and childhood experiences contributing to their unhealthy relationships. So where do you start the healing process? First you must identify the issues and become honest and open with yourself. Even in the matter of promiscuous individuals, there are issues contributing to such sexual behavior. Most people who live promiscuous lives have suffered from some sort of sexual abuse. Often this abuse occurs at a very young age, which perverts the image of sex. This refers to both men and women coping with suppressed emotions.

I looked back over my life and realized I didn't have things together and that's why I ended up hurt multiple times. Have you ever asked yourself, "How in the world did I end up here?" This often happens when you're in a vulnerable state. Love is cutthroat and the damage is underestimated. That's why a past relationship can affect a future one. Many people are guilty of holding onto past hurts from unhealthy relationships and end up with insecurities that threaten a healthy relationship. I'm guilty of that myself, but with the help from God, you can love and trust again.

Many times I feel as though we are so impatient. By being impatient we try to handle things on our own. Big mistake; when we do things on our own it ends up in a big mess that we expect God to clean up. There are so many people that end up with the wrong person because they didn't wait on God. Impatience will have you picking your partner instead of you waiting and letting God prepare you for who you're really supposed to be with. That's why there are so many unhappy marriages. I'll put it plain and simple--ya'll ain't supposed to be together." I'm here to tell you that marriage without God is no marriage. Now I know that statement alone is going to have all kinds of people writing me but it's true and I'll say it again. Marriage without God is no marriage. Couples become so desperate; I guess God was taking too long to find their soul mate, so they decide to find their own mate. When we try to work things out on our own, life ends up a hot mess and we wonder why. Even in the case of making hasty decisions, God can still make things work out in your favor. Many of you are guilty of having God clean up your mess all the time. However it all comes with a price, we still have to live with consequences of making bad decisions. During the cleaning up process God will teach you some things that will mature you. Are you willing to be made? Are you willing to be corrected?

We sometimes tend to think that we know what's best for our lives. God will always prove us wrong. Okay, maybe I'm just speaking from my own experience. When I tried to do things my way it was a mess. Maybe I'm the only person in this world that tried to do things their way. I don't know but, I'm just saying. I tried doing things my own way, and ended up all messed up and confused. God was clearly missing from the equation. At a young age I entered into a marriage filled with infidelity, lying, sneaking, and some more worldly things. Now you tell me, what in the world did I know about marriage at the age of seventeen? The answer to that question is NOTHING! If you don't think being unequally yoked is real, you better ask somebody. Again, that's what I chose. Somewhere down the line I knew that if God was not in it, the marriage would fail. I remember praying, "Lord whatever is in my life, which is keeping me from getting closer to you, I don't want it, Lord…take it away". As a result to that prayer, my life started to change and shift. I knew that change wouldn't be easy but it was definitely necessary.

Divorce is often frowned upon and I completely understand why. First of all, no one wants to get divorced. Getting divorced is not a trip that's pleasant. It can make you feel as though you were sleeping with the enemy. You sometime may see the worst come out of that person you once wanted to spend the rest of your life with. Also you may see the worse come out of you. Not only that, but if children are involved it's traumatic for them as well. Children get caught up in the midst and feel as though they have to choose sides. Though our sins are forgiven, our actions still lead to consequences. When vows are broken, trust is no longer there, and having a marriage without God, is a recipe for disaster and marriage can become very difficult. I'm not encouraging divorce in any way. That's a decision that I made after praying and studying the Bible for myself. You can judge me if you'd like, but that's a decision I made after taking my situation to God. I answer to God and God alone. However I do encourage anyone reading this book that may be seeking a divorce to take it up with God and not to let anyone else influence your decision.

My new chapter of love begins, or should I say picked up, where it left off. At the age of fourteen I found myself deeply in love. I had puppy love that wouldn't last, or so I was told. It was so

Marita Kinney   Why You're Still Single | 48
                              Chapter 18: My Experience with Love

strange to have the feelings I had. I wasn't sure what my feelings meant at the time. All I knew was that I enjoyed every minute of being in the company of this person. We had a connection and bond that seemed impossible to be broken. Even as a teenager, our relationship was very complicated. Even through many complications the bond was still there. I was at the age where I was seeking attention and had very low self-esteem. I didn't look like most girls my age. I was a lot smaller and it took me longer to develop physically. Most boys my age weren't interested in a relationship with me. I was "little Marita" to them, or referred to as "Westley's little sister". Either way, that meant I wasn't turning any heads. My parents always told me how beautiful I was, but I wasn't sure that I believed them. The boys didn't like me and had no idea who I'd grow up to be. I entered into a relationship with a young man that showed me attention and was known to be a nice guy. He played football and didn't get into trouble. There was no real commitment, but everyone knew that we were together. He never wanted to give us a title, although I desired one.

As years went by and I relocated, I wrote him once a year and never got one letter written back. It was clear to me that it was over and not worth holding onto. We lost all contact and moved on with our separate lives. I always wondered about him, and how life was with him. From time to time people from back home would mention his well-being to me and I have always prayed for his happiness. I knew this was a good person and that he would make someone very happy one day, if he in fact would actually commit to them. At the time I was married and limited my thoughts about him. You know how the enemy does, when things are rocky. He tries to make you think of things that you have no business thinking of. As the years went by and I began to mature and change, so did my circumstances. After talking with a cousin from my home town and realizing that he was extremely close to my first love, I was destined to be back in his life as a friend. Due to the lack of confidence that I once had, I felt that he mistreated me. I always knew that he loved me, but as with most teenage guys do, he had a hard time showing affection publicly. Being in love as a teenager was difficult, having feelings that were unexplainable. I later learned that you teach people how to treat you. Some issues occurred merely because I had no standards. I later held a grudge against him and wanted to apologize for also mistreating him as my form of retaliation. All I wanted was to ask for forgiveness, in spite of how he once treated me. Don't get me wrong, he was never a bad guy. He just didn't give me the recognition and commitment I felt was deserved. I was head over heels in love with him in high school and had no idea what an adult relationship with him would be like. I was no longer a child. I had grown into a confident woman with very high standards. Being divorced with two kids, a relationship was the last thing on my mind. Between work, kids, and church, there was really not any time for dating. By this time, I came to terms with the fact that I was very unique in the dating scene anyway. Men found it strange that I'd rather focus on my relationship with God than anything else. Not only that but I never took money from a man. So if money was all they had to offer me then they ended up confused. Being single after a divorce, I realized how superficial people were. Most men were only physically attracted to me and had no desire to see who I really was or what I had to offer. The things I desired in a man were rare and hard to find. I wanted someone who could love me for me, not my looks. Wisdom taught me that your appearance will change, and if a relationship is founded solely on looks, you're already setting yourself up for failure.

After contacting my first love to congratulate him for completing college, instantly we realized how much we both missed our friendship. Months passed from talking every now and again, and our friendship was again established. As my friend, he would even offer love advice to me. That was weird coming from him, but I valued his opinion. We later discussed what happened with us and agreed to try a relationship again. I was happy to have my friend and first love back in my life. It was challenging, but we worked at it and later were married. Not only were we married we were happy and had a daughter together. I knew he really loved me and it wasn't just because he found me to be attractive. He knew "me" and loved "me".

I was now with a man that loved God and it was great knowing that we had the same belief system, unlike my previous failed marriage. He often expressed that he felt as if I were a lot further in my walk with Christ. I explained how walking with Christ was a journey and people are at different places in their walk at different times. Through my life experiences, I became closer to God and it wasn't fair to compare each other's walk. Throughout the marriage he continually grew spiritually, but I often became discouraged because I felt that spiritually I was still leading the family. Reality was, he was still a babe in Christ and I found myself with unrealistic expectation for him.

In the beginning of 2009, I was about to have my first book published, the original version of "The Unspoken Walk." Life was good and I was ready to see the effects that the book would have on the world. I was sitting in the hospital room the day before Valentine's Day, with my husband who had a fever greater than 104 degrees. He was transferred there from another hospital after being said to have had sudden renal failure. The cause of his sudden illness was not yet identified. After a couple weeks of him believing he had the flu and being sent home from the ER on numerous occasions, the doctor at this new hospital was finally going to tell us what was wrong. This was a busy time of year for me, as I was patiently waiting to hear from my publisher about the release date of my book.

The doctor walked into the room. By this time the family had been moved to a special room. From the looks of the room you can tell it was designed comfortably with the purpose of delivery bad news. The doctor began to speak regretfully that the cause of illness was cancer, stage four NK (natural killer) cell leukemia. This was no ordinary cancer, but one that was very aggressive and he was the only one in the country with it. This news was astonishing. I could not believe that they were giving him only two weeks to live. After being told that devastating news, to my surprise my cell phone rang. It was my publisher telling me that my book was being released into the market. Talk about a bittersweet moment. Actually I could not realize the sweet, because this book was the last thing on my mind. Life was falling apart right before my eyes. I couldn't believe this was happening. After all the storms and trials that I had already faced, this didn't make sense. I wasn't a friend of death, although my entire life seemed to be centered around it. All the men in my life were leaving me. My brother was murdered, my father died from diabetes, I had already married young and divorced by the time I was twenty two, and now my husband is dying. Lord God, please keep me near the cross, because this I didn't understand.
As time went on, he lived four more months and then God called him home. I found him dead in our bedroom. He was sent home on hospice, and there his mother and I took turns caring for him. I remember praying each night asking God for strength for the following morning as I knew the day would come that he would part from this earth. I watched him slowly deteriorate. During his hospital stay, I practically lived at the hospital. I wasn't at home

with my children, as I felt obligated as a wife to be by his side. Family members were taking turns watching the children and I'd see them on the weekends. Meanwhile his family members and I were in rotation, vowing to never leave him alone to die. Someone was always there with him. I can remember countless times feeling homeless, being miles away from home and having to wash in public restroom sinks and never having privacy. It was all worth it, and I knew that God was still preparing me to become what He desired. *I Thessalonians 5:16-18 says, "Be joyful always; pray continually; give thanks in all circumstances, for this is God's will for you in Christ Jesus."*

During that time, those four months seemed like years. Time went by so slow and I was emotionally, physically, and mentally drained. My mother called me from Virginia and wanted to offer me some words of encouragement, because her heart ached for me and my situation. I agreed that I needed any amount of strength that would help me. She began to offer these amazing words of encouragement and tears just streamed down my face as I sat in the hospital hallway just feet away from the chapel where I'd go to pray. As I wiped my face, she asked if any of that sounded familiar to me and I replied no ma'am. She then told me, "Marita, I'm reading you the words from your book." I froze with a look of confusion that fell upon my face, as if forgetting that I had even written a book. That's how good God is. This book that was written just to help others, God knew that one day this book would also be written to help minister to me.

God gave me the strength that I'd prayed for and the courage to keep living. I could have checked out and given up on life. No, but I was determined to live and not be bitter. I had no idea that people wanted me to stay stuck in life. Many people were opposed to me moving on with life and could not understand how I could genuinely smile. They weren't able to walk in my shoes, therefore I had to understand their confusion. I cherished life and I refused to settle for that being all that God had for me. Something in my spirit told me that my life was just getting started, and that through my testimony, was healing for others. *Philippians 4:7 "And the peace of God, which surpasses all understanding, will guard your hearts and your minds in Christ Jesus."*

It was my assignment to literally love someone to death. It was an honor to have that humbling experience. *God trusted me to go through that.* Before we married he was a babe in Christ and he died a man of God, a firm believer in Christ. Was it possible that God allowed us to marry, to help him get closer to Christ? Could God have allowed me as the wife to influence him in such a way that he desired to strengthen his walk with Christ? Was it possible that God had me for him, so that he would have a praying wife by his side as he died? Did God have someone else ordained for me to actually grow old with? I did my job as a wife and I knew that God would honor my obedience and faithfulness. The enemy wanted to make me believe that God had forgotten about me, that I was abandoned by God. I loved someone with all my heart and at the age of twenty-six I was left a widow with three small children. Two children were from my previous marriage, and now my youngest was left completely fatherless. I needed God more now than ever before. Life was kicking my butt and I felt that my life was cursed. God then began to show me that He was still with me and was preparing me for something greater.

In Loving Memory of Franco Harden
6/14/2009

After a courageous battle with cancer
www.bethematch.com

I was being made into a true woman of God and was starting to believe what my father was trying to teach me. As I continued to trust God with my life, I had to often remind myself that His plan is perfect. Though I didn't understand what was shifting in my life, I felt the transition. God was showing me that my life's tragedies weren't personal at all. God knew that I'd come through them all stronger than I'd entered into them. He was preparing me to minister and to relate to His hurting people. I thank God for trusting me to love Him even through my pain, praising Him through my trials, and honoring Him in spite of my circumstances.

Love indeed hurts, but I wanted what God had for me. The million dollar question was, "If God allowed me to love again, would I be willing?" At one point I wasn't sure. The amazing thing is, the more I knew God and spent time with Him, the less I was angry at my situation of being alone and becoming a widow. God may have more for you, but will you welcome it? I began to welcome and accept my new life. I was determined to live and be happy. My children didn't deserve a bitter and angry black woman as their mother. I wanted to become the best woman I could be, not allowing my past to define me. I was ready to see what God had in store for me. After all, He told me this was just the beginning of my life. Today I'm happily married to Min. Demoine Kinney and he is a true gift from God. I never thought I'd meet someone that loved God as much as my father. My husband is a true man of God and he leads our family as God leads him. Some of you must think, "How is it that you were able to remarry?" That's simple, because I had peace with knowing that I was a good wife to my late husband. I had no regrets, I honored my vows, and was by his side until he took his last breath. God allowed me to have peace because of how I treated him during and even before his illness. I don't think that anyone can fully understand unless they had to watch someone they loved live in pain and die before their very eyes. To lose someone to an illness, is like having someone die before they actually leave this earth. I lost my late husband way before he died. I had to learn how to meet his needs as his needs changed. I became his caregiver, and continued to talk to him as if he was well. The illness took his strength, but I would not allow it to take his dignity. When you're faithful and honor God, He's faithful to you and I believed that God would give me the desire of my heart, to not grow old alone and for my children to have a father that serves God. God has smiled upon me and my family. I don't mean to brag, but my husband is the bomb and God knew exactly what I needed. I'm thankful for my husband, for loving me and taking me with all my scars, wounds, and insecurities. I'm not perfect, but I'm blessed. My husband made it a priority to show me things in life that I had never experienced. For the first time in my life, I had the chance to ride in a limousine and I wasn't on my way to a loved one's funeral. My husband was taking our family out to dinner. I'm now learning to live until I die. I'm still here, and life is still in me.

For those of you who have given up on love, keep the faith and your blessing is right around the corner. As I have shared some of my experiences with you, you can clearly see how I could have thrown in the towel on love. All odds were against me. I was previously divorced, became a widow, and was a mother to three children. Although that was all true, I had very high standards and knew that God wanted nothing but the best for me. I was never willing to settle for an average man, but I knew that God had prepared a king for me and that I was prepared to be his queen.

When I first met my husband, I knew there was something different about him. Even before we exchanged words, I could feel that God was doing something. I was at a place in life where I was tired of being hurt by love and was starting to become comfortable living as a single woman with children. I thank God that I was not bitter, because honestly, what man wants a bitter woman? FYI, that's just not attractive. After my late husband died, there were other men that had shown interest in me, but I thank God for the spirit of discernment.

After working with my husband for over two months on a Christian stage play, we finally exchanged words the last night of the performance. As the cast and crew members exchanged their cards to keep in touch, I wondered if he'd give me his card. Indeed he did, and we continued to keep in touch. As we learned more about each other, we noticed that we had a lot in common and experienced similar hurts. For the first time, I felt that someone really understood me. As we began to date, I realized that he not only was getting to know me, but he was studying me. He was so connected to me and could feel what I was feeling without me even saying a word. This caught me off guard as I'd never experienced this.

I had to remind myself that it was okay for him to love me. I struggled with the thought of someone else loving me at first. I knew that there was so much that went into being with me and often doubted if I deserved love again and if *I* deserved this awesome man. I wanted the relationship, but didn't want the disappointment that often follows love. When he disclosed his birthday to me, I was in disbelief to know that it was October 20th, the date my brother was killed. I then remembered how short life was and I was willing to go for the ride. Love hurts, but I was willing to take the risk. Demoine and I became very close and were falling in love. I knew that I was a good woman and stopped doubting my worth. Yes I had issues, yes I was a single parent, yes I had been a teenage mom, yes I went through a divorce, yes I was a widow, and yes I still knew that the woman God had developed me to be, was also a powerful woman of God that had wisdom and life experience. See some of you have given up, but I'm a fighter. I knew that God was making me into someone awesome. Satan will use your past against you, but my God will use your past to build you, shape, and mold you into something beautiful. My husband and I serve God together and both are wowed at what God has done in our lives. He was made for me and I was made for him.

Don't for one second think that God does not want the best for you. He did it for me and He will also do it for you. I can't begin to tell you all the people that hated on me for having yet another good man in my life. Do not allow the opinions of others to keep you from your blessing. Sometimes it's the closest people to you which will discreetly want you to fail. I cannot begin to express to you how God has moved in my life, and my God is worthy to be praised.

My husband not only loves me but the love he has for our children is amazing. Yes you read correctly, I said our children. Don't settle for someone loving you and ignoring your children. If you already have children, your significant other should love all of you and your children are indeed part of you. I take my hat off to my husband. I know that he's able to love me because he truly loves God. I thank him for reminding me how good it feels to laugh and enjoy life. Know your worth and accept nothing less than the best. My God is a healer and will restore what was lost or taken. Trust God and his plans for you. Thank God for the heartache and for the people that have walked out of your life. Trust the people that God will bring into your life and the ones He decides to remove. God continues to take me to glory to glory, higher and higher when I choose to trust Him. I love who I am and who I am not. *Proverbs 31:10 "Who can find a virtuous woman? For her price is far above rubies."* Today I am happily married with six children.

Chapter 19: What Men Really Want in a Wife

Women have gotten it ALL WRONG

Most men want a woman to have strong motherhood characteristics. They are looking for women to be good mothers. Even if the woman is unable to have children, he wants her to still possess those qualities. I have researched countless articles and interviews and the majority of men wants someone who reminds them of their own mother. In most cases their mother is the most influential and respected woman they know. Therefore they sub cautiously desire those same qualities as they're mother when they search for their potential spouse.

Just so you know, I've listed some of the qualities of a good mother.

Always offering your love. Gives lots of hugs.
Trying to see things from your kid's point of view. Asking their opinion whenever it's possible or appropriate.
Patience. And then more patience on top of that.
Setting boundaries
Giving unconditional love.
Having one on one time
Be their parent, not their friend, for the first 18 years or so. Then you'll be their best friend for the rest of your lives when they hit about 20 and suddenly get what you did for them. It's pretty awesome.
Be willing to get peed, pooped, and vomited upon.
Having a sense of humor.

Balance.

Making sure you always do the best you can, admit when you're not, learn to do better, and follow through.

Being able to survive harsh conditions. All kinds of harsh conditions.

Relaxing a little.

Not freaking out about doing things perfectly or according to what everyone else says.

Getting some time away, so you can come back an even better parent.

Thinking first before you yell or hit, or learn to live with regret.

Always letting your children know when they do a good job.

      For those of you who already have children. Make sure that you are not neglecting your children for your single life. Men are paying attention to what kind of mother you are. When I met my husband I was a single/widowed woman. I had no idea until after we were married that he chose me to be his wife because he admired the type of mother I was to my children. I then later discovered that I reminded him of his own mother. This is not at all uncommon. Ladies think about it. Most women with men issues also had daddy issues. We desire to be with a man who reminds us of our own fathers or what we desired to have from him.

Chapter 20: Single Mothers

Being a single mom is hard, especially if you're trying to date. Your motherhood could affect your love life. Believe or not, what kind of mother you are matters to a man. Men admire mothers more than they may realize. After all, most men adore their own mothers. The worse mistakes you can make as a mother dating are:

Being Ashamed of your kids
Lacking confidence as a mother
Asking a man to buy them things prior to a commitment
Yelling at the kids during a conversation with your love interest
Talking badly about the father
Dating more than parenting
Wanting a husband but not wanting them to be a father figure (playing with the kid but have an issue with him correcting him/her.
Introducing multiple men to your child- use wisdom...every love interest does not need to meet your child...HUGE NO NO.
Separate your old life and new life. Keep your ex out of your love life. Set healthy boundaries. You do not need your ex's approval. He's the father of your child...NOT YOUR FATHER
Don't talk to your kid(s) about your love interest. Remember that you're still talking with a child and certain adult conversations should be avoided.
Do not show affection towards men in front of your children. Again use wisdom...what if the relationship doesn't work out? You don't want the kids to see mommy kissing another random guy.
If he doesn't like your kids, it's going to be hard for him to love them.

Raising BAD kids will also turn a man off. Good mannered children are a reflection of your morals and who you are when no one is looking. Children tell people more about us than we realize. A friend once told me that I'd never find a man because I had three small children. Hearing that hurt me to the core. However, I didn't accept that, nor did I believe it. Always consider the source. My friend was a married man who didn't want children, but his wife did...badly. I had to remember who was talking to me....someone who didn't want any children. I'm so glad that I didn't believe his point of view. Instead I stood firm on my own beliefs. I knew that I was a good woman, a good mother, and that I deserved to be loved and accepted.

Chapter 21: Bitter Blues

You cannot hide bitterness. It's strong and very noticeable to everyone around you. No one enjoys being around bitter people. Bitter people are extremely negative and appear to be angry at the world. They will find something wrong with any and everything. This is a common reason why a lot of women remain single. Dump anything that is preventing you from becoming free to live a life of joy and purpose. The first step is to get over the past and anything or anyone that has hurt you. The past is...THE PAST. Your future is waiting for you. Begin to be happy for others. Instead of comparing your life to others, try celebrating the accomplishments of your friends and family. Being supportive is a great way to get over bitterness. It may take some practice, but it will move you towards the right direction.

Sad Single Women are not attractive. People will enjoy being around you, whenever you ENJOY BEING AROUND YOU. You're not ready for marriage if you're waiting for a man to complete you or make you happy. **Happiness should be discovered prior to getting married.**

How often do you smile?
Do you enjoy alone time?
Have you reached any new goals?
How have you been preparing yourself to become a wife?
Are you jealous of others when they find true love?

Chapter 22: Socially Independent

This chapter may seem elementary but indeed it's circuital to master this area in your life. Single women have a tendency to occupy each other's time and companion needs without ever realizing it. Think about it, who do your share you day with? If you're like the majority of women, you may call up your friends whenever you've had a bad day, opinions regarding decision making, meeting up for dinner, attending events, and just killing time. It's kind of weird when you think about it, but it's typical. This is very unattractive to a man who is looking for a wife. He is not trying to date you and your friends. Actually if you're always with your friends, chances are that your guy may not ever approach you. Why? Because men don't like rejection. Women are more likely to reject a man if she is in the company of her friends. For some reason, we sometimes seek the approval of our friends. As mentioned in this book earlier, do not take advice from your single friends....remember their also single. They can give you advice that they wouldn't take themselves. I'm not suggesting that you end your social life. I'm merely advising you to shift your dependency of it. Woman who have a highly fulfilled social life are often times single women. Those women are freely available to be that social butterfly that they are. They key word is single woman. Married women are a bit more socially independent. They may also attend events, but they do so in different fashion. They may arrive separately than their friends, may not stay the whole time, and may not attend events as often as single women. Remember you have to create the lifestyle you desire. Wives have other priorities. Constantly hanging out with their friends could compromise her relationship if there isn't any balance.

Now, let's take it a step further. Are your friends keeping you single? Think about how much time they take up in your day. It's all about balance and becoming independent of them. Have you ever had a friend that you used to hear from and hang out with until they got a man? That happens because it's difficult to have a relationship and maintain your friends on the same time consuming level. Ok, enough of that. I'm sure you get the point. I'm going to now be brutally honest with you. Whenever I see a group of women that are regularly together, I think of women who will remain single for a longer period of time. I'm not trying to be judgmental, it's just not necessary for a gown woman to consistently be in the company of other women. A grown confident woman should be able to always stand alone and be ok. It's more attractive to a man. If you don't believe me I dare you to ask ten men. Women who are socially independent have a better chance of getting married. Here's why. Rejection! There's that word goes again.

Imagine a man walking into a coffee shop and noticing a group of women. You see him and hope that maybe he'll come your way. You pretend to be engaged in the conversation with your friends, but you're actually waiting to see what this attractive man's next move will be. Here are the scenarios that could take place.

Scenario 1: The man notices a woman sitting alone and she finds favor in his eyes. They exchanged smiles and before you know it, she has his undivided attention. This woman was
Available for his conversation
Less likely to reject his interest
And was not distracted from the company of her friends

Scenario 2: The man notices you and you two exchange smiles. He's brave enough to approach you and your friends and starts a friendly conversation. This is a lot of pressure because he has to entertain all of you. Let's say that you're a little reserve and one of your friends is more outgoing. She begins to flirt with the guy and before you know it, her flattery took his attention off of you and he is now interested in her. Why? Because he understands her interest, she boldly makes it clear and doesn't have to risk being rejected by her.

Those are just a couple of situations that could have played out for the purpose of proving my point. A group of women could be intimidating for a man to approach. Most men would rather communicate with you one on one. So if you happen to be with some friends and notice a man's strong interest in you, try to position yourself in a manner that is less intimidating for him. I'm not trying to dictate your life, I am simply sharing this with you to keep in mind.

Think about all of the single women you know. How socially independent are they? How independent are you socially? Even single mothers have an advantage in this area. Motherhood has a way of changing your prospective on life. Single moms may not have as many friends to hang out with, nor the extra time to waste. I remember after I became a widow some single women began to invite me to several functions. They were not my friends, but they assumed that I would have a good time with them. Although I was newly single, I was still a mother and lacked the deposable time. I'll never forget the last few events that they invited me to. One happen to be a sleepover. From my perspective there was no way I was attending that. To pay for a babysitter just to sleep on somebody's floor, did not seem appealing to me. I had other obligations and my free time was important to me. I chose not to spend my time sleeping over at someone else's home, with a pillow and change of clothes. I then realized that I was different. I was socially independent. I had friends of course, but we all had something in common. We could also stand alone. We didn't talk every day, we didn't live our lives on Facebook, and we all had a life outside of our friendship. By the way, the women who invited me to those events are still single. Maybe by choice or default, I'm not sure, but nevertheless single.

Friendships have to have boundaries. They should not have the same privileges as your husband. Once you get married, how will your marriage be different then your friendships? Of course sex, but is there anything else? There has to be a clear distinction. Begin to separate your friends from being involved in everything that you do. Decide what you would like to share with them and what you're reserving for your future companion. Begin to practice your independency from them now to avoid possible issues later.

Tips From A Married Woman

Have high standards but minimal exceptions until you have a commitment. (Men do not like pressure or a demanding woman. Disappointment follow expectations

- Don't compare relationships (Men don't need details a about your past love interest. Even if he ask, keep it minimal and don't reveal too much. Keep the past in the past

- Smell good all the time. Including your hair. Men like smells and foul odors is a huge turn off.

- Don't be readily available. That's a sure sign of desperation. When on the phone hung with a guy be the first to hang up, or miss a few calls when calls you. After all you have a life too and can't talk all the time…right?

- Stroke his ego. Men love compliments and words of affirmation

- If you don't believe in his dreams, he is not the man for you. Men want support. If you don't believe in him, you'll hurt him and not realize it.

- Ditch your phone. Being married to your phone will leave you single.

- Mind your own business. Woman who gossip about their friends may have a man question your loyalty.

- Listen! Really Listen. Instead of talking about yourself, listen and remind him at a later time that you indeed heard him.

- Earn his trust. A man wants to trust you with his heart.

- Encourage him. Believe in him even when he has doubts.

- Be ladylike. Don't allow men to view you as their homeboy. Always earn the respect of being a woman.

- Set goals. A lost woman is a lost cause. Know where you want to go and how you want to get there.

- Let some things go. Don't ponder on differences, only those that truly matter. Women who are argumentative seldom keep their man.

- Practice intimacy without sex. Talking is very sexy. I'm not referring to nasty conversation, but intellectual chats instead. Stimulate his mind…yep blow his mind with your conversation.

- Look at the cause instead of effects. Understand what makes the man who he truly is.

- Men marry wives before they're a wife. That means that you have to be and have a wife mentality while you're single.

- You can't buy sexy. Being sexy is a demeanor. It's in the way that you walk, speak, care for others, pray, and being confident in your own skin.

- Be THE ONE in order to attract THE ONE

Conclusion

Each love story is unique. It can take weeks (or months) before you fall in love with each other, or you may know that he's the right one on your first date. It may take him months or even years to ask you to marry him, or it may just happen in a matter of weeks. No matter what your love story ends up to be, have faith that it is bound to be beautifully written.

You've been on such a beautiful journey to rediscover yourself. No matter how hard it was, you faced your issues and dealt with them. Each step you took made you the woman that you are now. You made a decision to respect yourself. You've also thought about what you really need and want. You were willing to wait because you wanted nothing but the best for you.
It is our hope that the twelve-step guide we gave you has truly helped in getting you a great man who'd eventually marry you. Hopefully, the both of you would never forget to love and respect yourselves and each other.

However, reality is, we can't guarantee that every single relationship will work. Failed relationships are experiences and our experiences can be used as lessons to improve our lives. There are numerous factors that affect relationships. We've covered only one important factor, and that's you.

The good news is, no matter what happens in any of your relationships from here on, you'll know the importance of self-respect. You won't feel as if you've lost all the things that define you as an individual, simply because you've kept doing activities that make you a better person each day. You also know better now, and you really know what you need, want, and deserve.

If it didn't work out the way you hoped it would, don't worry. You're in a far better place now than when you've started. If you were with a great guy already, imagine how better your husband is going to be. Your goal now is to make new achievements endlessly. Never stop respecting yourself and every person you meet, and eventually you'd see the difference it has made in your life.

The most important step: Love God first

The best way to love you is to simply love God first. When you give and receive God's love, it spills over to others in your life; not only will you learn how to love yourself but how to also love others. "Love the Lord your God with all your heart and with all your soul and with all your strength and with all your mind; and, Love your neighbor as yourself." Luke 10:27

About the Author

Who is Marita Kinney? **Marita L Kinney** is an Amazon Best-Selling Author and a woman of many talents. A published Author, Life Coach and Motivational Speaker, Marita has inspired thousands of people to overcome adversity with triumph through faith and perseverance. While facing several life changing challenges herself, Marita had enough faith to conquer tribulations, coming out victorious. She is best known for her Christian Fiction novellas and heart felt inspirational books. Capturing the true essence of what it means to turn "lemons into lemonade", she has taken the harsh lessons of life and developed a plan for successfully living.

Marita is wife of Comedian, Actor, and Saxophonist, Demoine Kinney. They are the proud parents of six children.

Follow me on Twitter @MaritaKinney

www.MaritaKinney.com

Check Out My Other Books

Below you'll find some of my other popular books that are popular on Amazon and Kindle as well. Simply click on the links below to check them out. Alternatively, you can visit my author page on Amazon to see other work done by me

Not Tonight, I'm Tired

Sex and a Cup of Coffee

The Unspoken Walk

The Snow's Meltdown

Don't Rescue Me, God's Molding...

Seed Of Discord

Sasha

Who Will Hold My Bags

Simply search for these titles on the Amazon website to find them.

MANY MORE....

Signed! Today more and more people download books and don't have the opportunity to have them signed.

Thank you for your support and you do have a signed copy!!!

www.ingramcontent.com/pod-product-compliance
Lightning Source LLC
Chambersburg PA
CBHW031610040426
42452CB00006B/463